GET WELL SOON

Ear Infection

Anita Ganeri and

Beatriz Castro

Enslow PUBLISHING

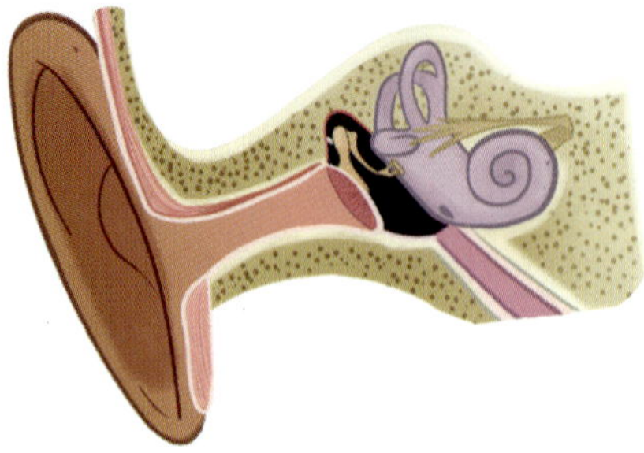

Published in 2025 by Enslow Publishing, LLC
2544 Clinton Street
Buffalo, NY 14224

First published in Great Britain in 2023 by Hodder & Stoughton

Series editor: Julia Bird
Illustrator: Beatriz Castro
Design: Collaborate

Manufactured in the United States of America

CPSIA compliance information: Batch #CSENS25: For further information contact Enslow Publishing LLC, New York, New York at 1-800-398-2504.

Please visit our website, www.enslowpublishing.com. For a free color catalog of all our high-quality books, call toll free 1-800-398-2504 or fax 1-877-980-4454.

Cataloging-in-Publication Data

Names: Ganeri, Anita, 1961-. | Castro, Beatriz.
Title: Ear infection / by Anita Ganeri and Beatriz Castro.
Description: Buffalo, NY : Enslow Publishing, 2025. | Series: Get well soon
Identifiers: ISBN 9781978538627 (pbk.) | ISBN 9781978538634 (library bound) | ISBN 9781978538641 (ebook)
Subjects: LCSH: Otitis media in children--Juvenile literature.
Classification: LCC RF225.G24 2025 | DDC 618.92'09784--dc23

GET WELL SOON

Ear Infection

Hi! My name is Jan, and this book is all about the time I got an ear infection. My ears hurt, and I felt really awful. The doctor looked in my ears to see what was wrong. But after a few days I felt much better again.

This book has information and advice about getting an ear infection to help you and your parents or caregivers. On the following pages, you can find out:

What is an ear infection?

How do you get one?

Why do your ears hurt?

What makes you feel better?

This book is about an illness called an ear infection. Lots of children get ear infections, especially after they've had a cold or the flu.

It's the morning of the class's weekly music lesson.
Everyone has been looking forward to it.
They love making noise!

Jan missed last week's lesson because he had a cold and had to stay at home. He's happy today because he can play the drums.

Jan and his friends go into the music room. There are all sorts of different musical instruments in the room.

Jan heads straight to the drums. He loves playing the drums. He takes lessons after school.

At the beginning of the school year, Jan and his class listened to lots of different pieces of music. Then they voted for the three pieces they liked best. They've been practicing a lot. They're nearly ready to play for their parents at the end-of-year concert.

Today, they're rehearsing their first song. It's Jan's favorite because there's a drum solo, and he'll be playing it!

Mr. Balik starts playing the introduction on the piano. Then the class joins in. Sophia smiles at Tom – his violin is perfectly in tune, luckily.

The class start the piece all over again. Everyone is on time. Soon, it's time for the drum solo. Miss Lindsay calls Jan's name to remind him, but there's no reply. She tells the class to stop playing.

Mr. Balik takes Jan to see the school nurse. Jan tells the nurse that his ears are hurting, and he can't hear very well. The nurse takes his temperature.

Mr. Balik calls Jan's dad, and he comes to take Jan home. He tells Jan that he has made an appointment for him to see the doctor the next day.

He asks Jan if he wants some lunch, but Jan isn't hungry. He tells his dad that he feels a bit sick, and that chewing makes his ears hurt more.

Jan's mom takes him to the doctor the next morning. The doctor asks Jan how he is feeling. She looks inside his ear with a special instrument called an otoscope.

It shines a light into Jan's ear so the doctor can see inside. It also blows a small puff of air.

The doctor finishes her examination. She tells Jan that he has an ear infection and asks him if he has had a cold recently. Ear infections are very common when you've had a cold. They're caused by germs, like the viruses that cause colds and flu, and sometimes by bacteria too.

The doctor shows Jan and his mom a diagram of the inside of an ear.

The eustachian tube normally lets any fluid in the middle ear drain away to the back of the throat. But when you have a cold, the tube swells and gets blocked. This means fluid builds up in your ear and presses on your eardrum, which is very painful.

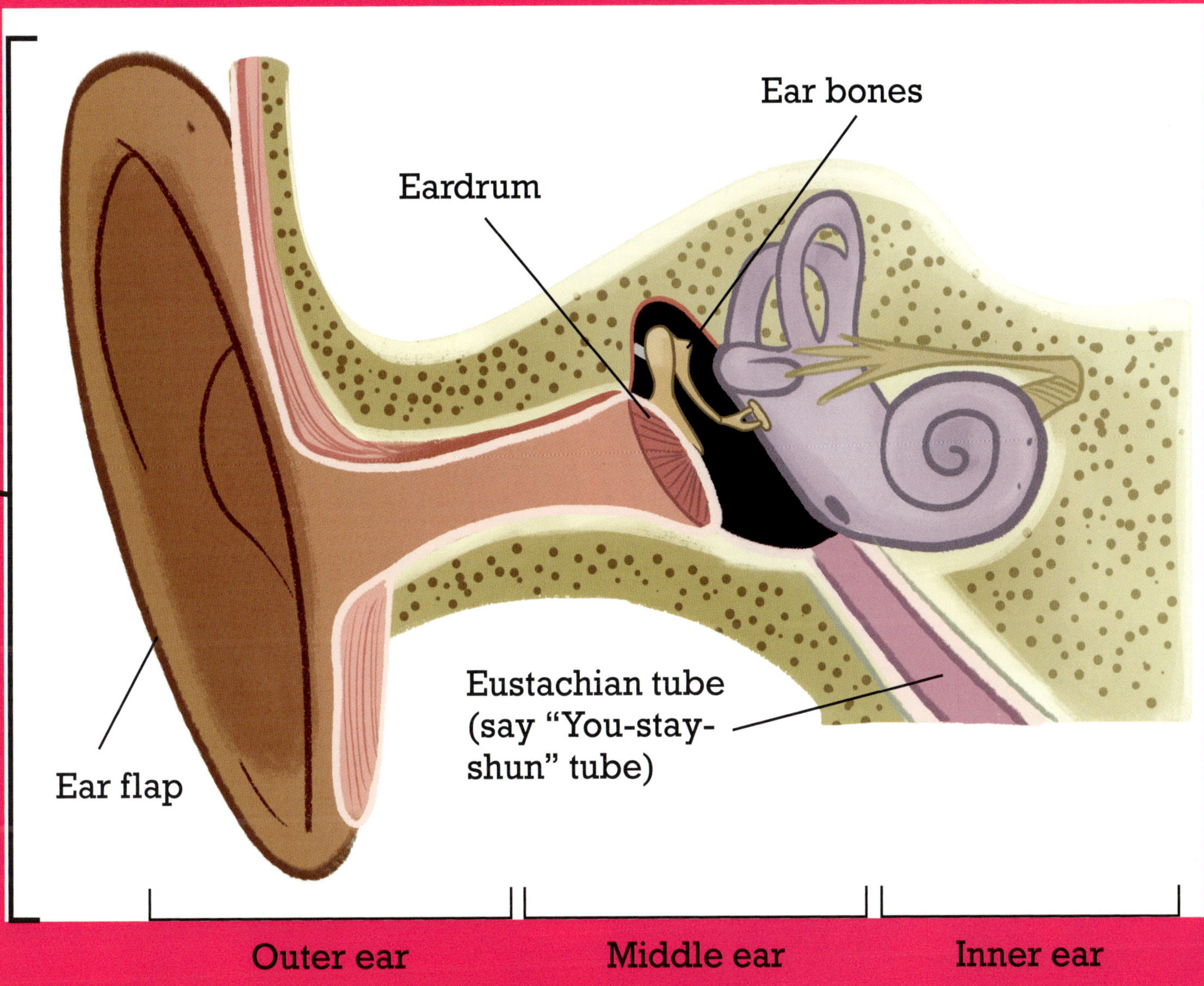

DID YOU KNOW?

Children get more ear infections than adults because the tubes in their ears are shorter and narrower. The tubes let germs in more easily, and are more likely to get blocked.

Ear infections are very common illnesses, especially when you're young. But how do you know if you've got one? Here are some clues to look out for. Clues that tell you about an illness are called symptoms. The symptoms of an ear infection often come on very quickly.

If you've got these, you may have an ear infection. A doctor will be able to tell you for sure. But don't worry – you should be feeling better soon.

The doctor prescribes Jan some antibiotics for his ear infection. She tells him to come back to see her if he's not feeling better in a few days.

ANTIBIOTICS

While it's possible an ear infection could get better on its own, it's likely a doctor will give you a kind of medicine called an antibiotic. This will help kill any bacteria that might be causing your ear infection. Antibiotics don't kill viruses (the germs that cause colds and flu).

Back home, Dad sends Jan to bed to get some rest. He gives Jan some acetaminophen (there's a special liquid type for children). It helps to make Jan's ears less painful.

Dad knows how worried Jan is about missing the concert. He goes downstairs and turns on his computer. He looks for any other ways to help Jan get better. He finds some useful advice on a website that the doctor recommended.

After a few days, Jan is feeling much better. His ears don't hurt anymore, and he can hear again.

Back at school, Miss Lindsay is very happy to see Jan. Today is the last music lesson before the concert. Everything needs to be perfect.

This time, Jan comes in for his drum solo – right on time!

QUIZ

Now that you've reached the end of the book, how much do you think you know about ear infections? Try this quick quiz to find out.

1. What are some signs of an ear infection?
a) High temperature
b) Painful ears
c) Headache

2. When might you get an ear infection?
a) When you're feeling tired
b) When you've had a cold
c) When you've bumped your head

3. Why do ear infections happen?
a) Tubes inside your nose get blocked
b) Tubes inside your throat get blocked
c) Tubes inside your ears get blocked

4. How long does it usually take for an ear infection to clear up?
a) A few weeks
b) A few hours
c) A few days

5. What shouldn't you do to feel better?
a) Take acetaminophen
b) Poke something in your ear
c) Get water in your ear

Answers:
1. All three; 2. b); 3. c); 4. c); 5. b) & c)

USEFUL WORDS

acetaminophen
Medicine used to treat aches and pains.

antibiotic
A medicine used to treat infections by bacteria.

bacteria
Types of germs that can get inside your body and make you ill.

diagram
A detailed picture with labels to show how something works.

eardrum
The thin flap of skin stretched tight like a drum inside your ear.

Eustachian tube
The tube inside your ear that connects with your throat.

germs
Very small living things that can cause illnesses.

otoscope
An instrument doctors use to look inside your ears.

solo
When you play part of a piece of music on your own.

viruses
Types of germ that can get inside your body and make you ill.

MORE INFORMATION

WEBSITES

https://kidshealth.org/en/kids/ear-infection.html?ref=search
Lots of information for you about ear infections.

https://kidshealth.org/en/parents/infections/ear?ref=search
Lots of information for your parents or caregivers about what to do if you get an ear infection.

BOOKS

All About Ear Infections by Francesca Potts, RN (Abdo Publishing, 2018)

Germs by Anna Claybourne (Gareth Stevens, 2025)

ADVICE FOR PARENTS AND CAREGIVERS

This book is about a type of ear infection, called otitis media, which affects the middle ear, behind the eardrum. The middle ear is linked to the back of the nose by the Eustachian tube. Otitis media is very common in children, and can often follow colds or the flu.

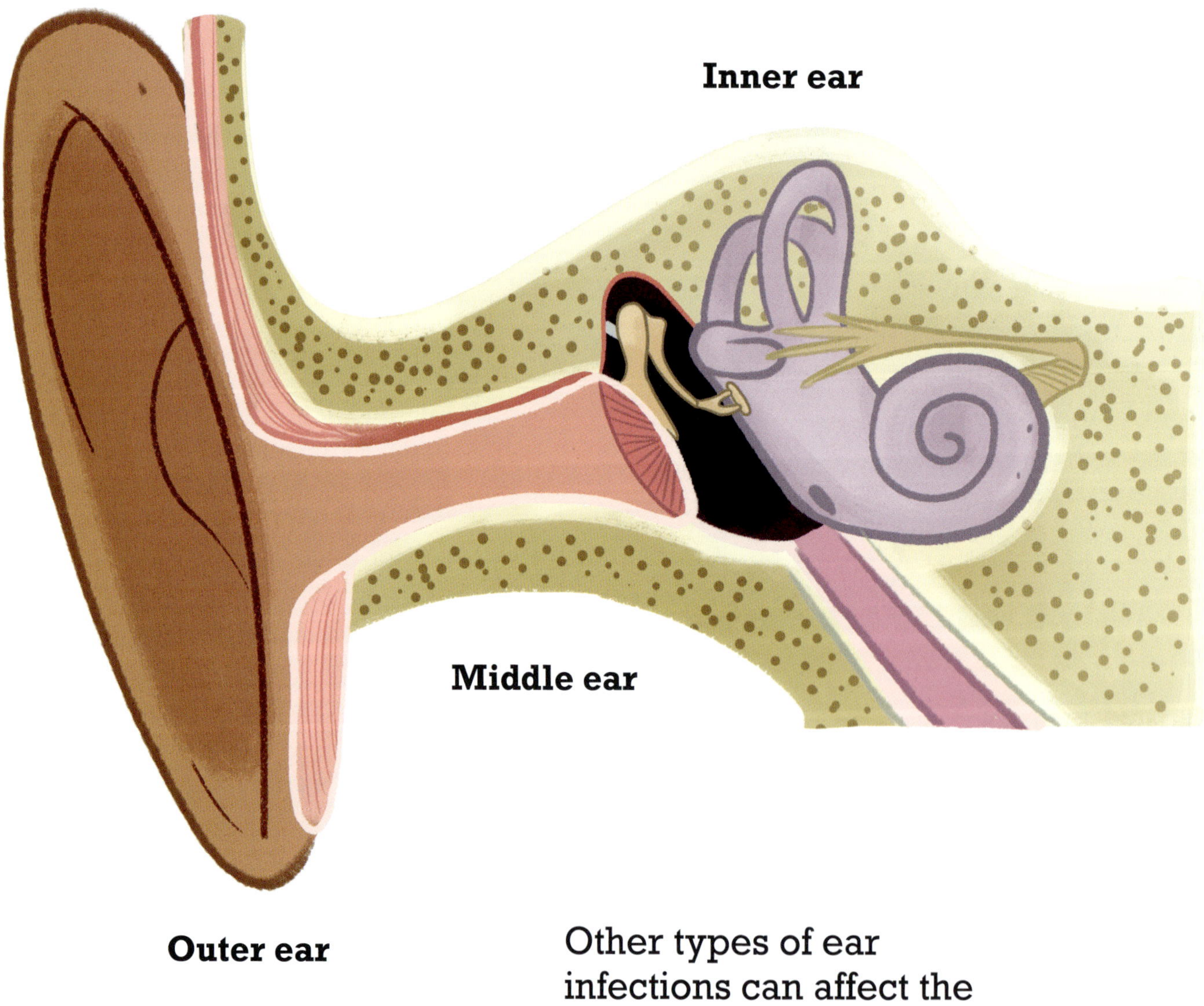

Other types of ear infections can affect the outer and inner ear.

WATCH OUT FOR VIRUSES

Ear infections are most common in autumn and winter, when people are more likely to catch colds or the flu. Ear infections themselves aren't contagious, but the colds and and the flu that cause them can be. Viruses can easily be spread to other people in coughs and sneezes, so children should be encouraged to use a tissue, and to wash their hands regularly.

GROWING UP

Young children get more ear infections than adults because their Eustachian tubes are shorter and more horizontal (see page 19) and they tend to get more viral infections generally. Very young children may get repeated middle ear infections, but these usually get less frequent as the child gets older.

INDEX